My World
Your World

The Food We Eat

by Ellen Lawrence

Ruby Tuesday Books

Published in 2015 by Ruby Tuesday Books Ltd.

Copyright © 2015 Ruby Tuesday Books Ltd.

Editor: Mark J. Sachner
Designer: Emma Randall
Production: John Lingham

Photo credits:
Alamy: 4, 6 (top), 9, 10 (left), 16 (top), 17, 19 (left), 21, 22; Corbis: 8 (left), 19 (right), 22; FLPA: Cover, 2, 5, 12–13, 15, 22; Shutterstock: 5, 6 (bottom), 7, 8 (right), 10 (right), 11, 14 (left), 14 (right: Claudio Zaccherini), 16 (bottom), 18, 20 (africa924), 22, 23.

British Library Cataloguing In Publication Data (CIP) is available for this title.

ISBN 978-1-910549-53-7

Printed in India

www.rubytuesdaybooks.com

The picture on the front cover of this book shows people enjoying a winter barbecue in Sweden.

Contents

Words shown in **bold** in the text are explained in the glossary.

All the places in this book are shown on the map on page 22.

What Foods Do We Eat?

It's porridge for breakfast in Namibia.

A delicious dinner of vegetables and noodles in the United States.

A school lunch of sausage and chips in Germany.

Durian fruit

Fruit is a popular food all over the world.

In Malaysia, many people eat durian fruit. This fruit smells like strong cheese and onions, but it tastes like custard. In Mexico, people eat black sapote fruit that tastes like chocolate.

Black sapote fruit

5

A Very Important Food

There is one food that people eat all over the world – rice.

Rice is a type of grass plant.

The rice grains we eat are the plant's seeds.

People grow and eat more than 40,000 different types of rice!

Rice grains

Rice krispie cakes made from puffed rice cereal

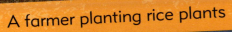
A farmer planting rice plants

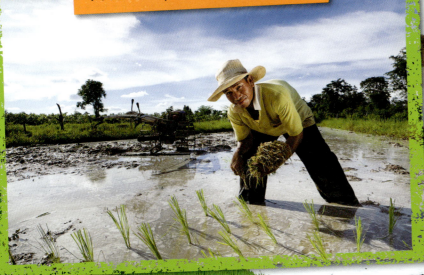

Rice plants grow best in places where the land is very wet. Often farmers flood their rice fields with water from nearby rivers.

Farmers ploughing their flooded fields with water buffaloes

Rice growing in flooded fields on a hillside in Vietnam

Delicious Bento Boxes

Every day, many children in Japan open their lunchboxes to see their favourite animal or cartoon character.

The colourful lunchboxes are called bento boxes.

Japanese mums turn food into animal faces, superheroes, cars, flowers and many other shapes.

A bento box

The food in a bento box usually includes rice balls, seaweed, mini hot dog sausages, hard-boiled eggs, cheese, **pickled** vegetables and fruit.

Seaweed

Rice ball

Hot dog sausage

Sweets for Diwali

The **festival** of Diwali is celebrated by Hindu, Sikh and Jain people around the world.

Diwali is also known as the festival of lights.

It celebrates the victory of light over darkness and of good over evil.

An oil lamp

People decorate their homes with small oil lamps.

They eat lots of homemade sweets and give boxes of sweets as presents.

Diwali sweets are made from many **ingredients**, including flour, beans, lentils, carrots, pumpkins, nuts, raisins and yogurt.

Food from a Forest

The Baka are a group of people who live in **rainforests** in Africa.

They hunt or find their food in the forest.

Baka men hunt for antelopes, crocodiles and monkeys.

Women and children catch fish, turtles, caterpillars and giant land snails to eat.

A giant land snail

Baka people find mushrooms and berries in the forest. They also search for beehives in trees. Then they gather the honey.

This Baka boy is licking honey from some honeycomb.

Food from Yaks

In Tibet, people raise hairy cattle called yaks.

Yak farmers get meat and milk from their yaks.

They make butter from yak milk.

Yak butter for sale in a market

People dry yak dung, or poo, and burn it as fuel for cooking and heating.

Yak dung

Yak butter is mixed with hot water, tea and salt to make a warming, fatty drink. Butter tea is the favourite drink of people in Tibet.

A yak pulling a sledge loaded with hay to feed the yak herd

Fish and Chips

In the United Kingdom, many people love to eat fish and chips.

It's **traditional** to eat this food on a Friday night.

People eat lots of extras with fish and chips such as mushy peas, gherkins and pickled onions.

Fish and chips

Mushy peas

A gherkin

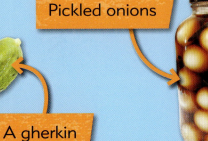

Pickled onions

In the UK, it's also traditional to eat fish and chips at the seaside.

Fasting for Ramadan

Ramadan is the holiest month of the year for Muslims.

During this time, people fast, or don't eat, between sunrise and sunset.

They say extra prayers and try to give up bad habits.

Fasting helps people remember that not everyone has enough to eat.

Many people stop their fast each evening by eating dates. Then families and friends gather for a meal called *iftar*.

Dates

A family eating
iftar in Indonesia

An iftar meal in the United Arab Emirates

No Food to Eat

Not everyone around the world has enough to eat.

Many people are too poor to buy food.

Many people live in places where they cannot grow food.

Every night, millions of adults and children go to bed hungry.

These people are looking for food on a rubbish dump.

In Brazil's cities, many children live on the streets. They sleep in cardboard boxes and search for food in dustbins. **Charities** try to bring food and drink to the street children.

Street children in Brazil eating food from charity workers

21

Where in the World?

United Kingdom
Pages 6 and 16–17

Germany
Page 4

Sweden
Front cover

United Arab Emirates
Page 19

Tibet, China
Pages 14–15

China
Page 6

Japan
Pages 8–9

North America

Europe

Asia

Africa

South America

Australia

Cameroon
Pages 12–13

Vietnam
Page 7

United States
Page 4

Mexico
Page 5

India
Pages 10–11

Indonesia
Page 19

Brazil
Page 21

Namibia
Page 4

Rwanda
Page 5

Mozambique
Page 20

Malaysia
Page 5

Glossary

charity
An organisation that raises money and uses it to do good work such as helping people living in poverty.

festival
A day or several days when a large number of people enjoy a celebration.

ingredient
A food or substance that is used to make a particular dish or meal. For example, flour, eggs and sugar are the main ingredients used to make a cake.

pickled
Put into vinegar or salty water. When foods are pickled it gives them a tangy taste and they last for a long time.

rainforest
A thick forest of trees and other plants where lots of rain falls.

traditional
Something that has been done in a certain way for many years by a group of people. For example, eating a particular type of food.

Index

Learn More Online

To learn more about food
around the world, go to
www.rubytuesdaybooks.com/food